CORGANICS

REVOLUTIONIZING HEALTHCARE WITH CLINICAL CANNABINOID THERAPY

BENCHMARK BOOKS

FREILING
AGENCY

Published by Freiling Agency, LLC.

P.O. Box 1264
Warrenton, VA 20188

www.FreilingAgency.com

PB ISBN: 978-1-963701-18-0
HB ISBN: 978-1-963701-17-3
E-book ISBN: 978-1-963701-19-7

CONTENTS

INTRODUCTION

Benchmark Books is a groundbreaking series dedicated to illuminating the stories and strategies of America's most remarkable companies.

A benchmark serves as a pivotal yardstick against which companies measure their progress and competitiveness. This essential tool provides a standardized point of reference, facilitating comparisons with industry peers, market norms, or internal targets. Whether assessing financial health, operational efficiency, product quality, or strategic alignment, benchmarks offer invaluable insights into organizational performance. By establishing clear benchmarks, companies gain the ability to pinpoint areas of strength, identify opportunities for improvement, and chart a course toward sustained success. In essence, benchmarks serve as navigational aids, guiding decision-making and driving continuous improvement in pursuit of excellence.

The purpose of Benchmark Books is to identify and document America's baseline companies with meticulous research, thorough investigation, and interviews with management, vendors, and customers. Benchmark Books delves into the inner workings of industry trailblazers, uncovering the secrets to their success and the visionary leadership behind their achievements. Through a rigorous benchmarking process, we meticulously compare and analyze companies within their respective industries, providing readers with unparalleled insights into best practices, competitive landscapes, and emerging trends.

With each volume, Benchmark Books offers a comprehensive roadmap for understanding, emulating, and ultimately surpassing the benchmarks set by these extraordinary organizations. We look for the best of the best, certain companies that stand out not just for their profitability or market dominance, but also for their unwavering vision, relentless innovation, and commitment to growth. These companies, often helmed by visionary founders, serve as an inspiration and model of success for aspiring entrepreneurs, investors, and seasoned professionals alike.

This book is the culmination of our endeavor to uncover and showcase the essence of an exceptional organization. Our criteria were stringent, focusing not solely on financial metrics but also on the holistic health and visionary leadership that propels these companies forward. Through a combination of rigorous research methodologies and firsthand accounts from key stakeholders, we have identified a select group of America's visionary companies. These are not merely enterprises; they are living entities with stories to tell, lessons to impart, and legacies to leave behind. From innovative startups disrupting industries to established titans charting new paths, the company featured in each book offers invaluable insights into what it takes to thrive in today's competitive marketplace.

Who is this book for? It is for the curious minds eager to understand the inner workings of America's most successful enterprises. It is for the aspiring entrepreneurs seeking inspiration and guidance on their journeys to greatness. It is for the seasoned executives and business leaders looking to glean fresh perspectives and strategies for sustainable growth.

Join us as we embark on a captivating exploration of America's visionary companies. Through these books, we invite you to discover the stories, strategies, and secrets that have propelled these organizations to the forefront of success!

Benchmarked: Corganics

Corganics® provides broad-spectrum CBD products and education to healthcare professionals and their patients. In January 2020, a cadre of pharmaceutical industry stalwarts embarked on a mission to redefine the landscape of holistic healthcare. Thus, Corganics® was born, with an ambitious aim to bridge the informational chasm separating healthcare professionals and their patients in understanding and leveraging the potential of the Endocannabinoid System (ECS). As patients across the United States increasingly seek safe, natural alternatives to traditional pharmaceuticals, Corganics emerged as a beacon of trust and innovation, offering a suite of scientifically formulated, physician-advised broad-spectrum CBD products that have swiftly garnered acclaim among healthcare professionals across myriad specialties.

At the heart of Corganics' ethos lies an unwavering commitment to excellence, underpinned by advanced technology, meticulous manufacturing processes, and stringent quality control measures. Set apart by a dedication to transparency and integrity, Corganics' products undergo exhaustive third-party testing and boast IRB-approved data, positioning them as the gold standard in an industry too often plagued by inconsistency and ambiguity.

Corganics' aspirations extend beyond mere product innovation. Recognizing the historical marginalization of healthcare professionals in conversations surrounding CBD therapy, the company has made it a core tenet to elevate their role as trusted, unbiased purveyors of knowledge. Through a concerted educational effort, Corganics seeks to empower healthcare professionals to navigate the complexities of hemp-derived cannabinoid therapy with confidence, elucidating its potential benefits and interactions with the ECS. In forging symbiotic partnerships with healthcare professionals, Corganics not only envisions a future of enhanced patient care but also a reimagined paradigm wherein holistic wellness and informed decision-making reign supreme.

When we visited Corganics® corporate headquarters in Dallas, Texas, we listened to the company's founders, met staff, reviewed financials, and took a deep dive into what makes the company tick. Our benchmarking process included asking tough questions:

- How does Corganics plan to differentiate itself from the increasingly crowded market of CBD products?

- With growing competition and regulatory challenges, how does the company ensure sustained profitability and growth?

- Can Corganics elaborate on its long-term vision for integrating hemp-derived cannabinoid therapy into mainstream healthcare practices?

- What specific steps is the company taking to achieve this vision, and how does it plan to navigate regulatory hurdles and public perception surrounding CBD products?

- What specific expertise or insights do the pharmaceutical industry executives bring to Corganics?

- How do their backgrounds uniquely position them to lead the company in addressing the challenges and opportunities inherent in the CBD industry?

- What investments is Corganics making in research and development to continually innovate its product offerings and stay ahead of emerging trends in cannabinoid therapy?

- Given the historical exclusion of healthcare professionals from conversations surrounding CBD therapy, what strategies is Corganics employing to educate and engage this crucial stakeholder group?

- How does the company plan to foster trust and credibility among healthcare professionals as a trusted source of information on cannabinoid therapy?

- How does Corganics ensure the quality and consistency of its raw materials and finished products throughout its supply chain?

- What measures are in place to mitigate risks associated with contamination, adulteration, or non-compliance with regulatory standards?

- What are Corganics' key performance indicators (KPIs) for measuring success, and how does the company track progress against these metrics?

- What are the company's growth projections for the coming years, and what factors could potentially impact its financial performance and market position?

This book includes the results of our research.

—Tom Freiling

1

THE INDUSTRY SETTING

In 1963, a young organic chemist working at a research university in Israel made an important discovery.

Working to better understand cannabis and how it affects the human body, he and his team determined the stereochemistry of cannabidiol, or CBD—a chemical found in the cannabis plant. CBD doesn't contain tetrahydrocannabinol (THC), the psychoactive ingredient found in marijuana that produces a high. With an eye toward eventual pharmacological applications, this important step in the study of what was (and remains) one of the world's most widely used drugs laid the groundwork for decades of research that continues to generate therapies for a spectrum of diseases and ailments—from epilepsy and schizophrenia to inflammation, chronic pain, and various types of cancer.

Today, both that university—the prestigious Weizmann Institute of Science in

Rehovat, Israel—and that scientist—Raphael Mechoulam—are household names in the fields of organic chemistry and pharmacology. Weizmann is universally renowned as one of the world's leading research universities, boasting six Nobel laureates and three Turing Award winners among its faculty. And in a 2023 obituary for Mechoulam, the *New York Times* hailed his "groundbreaking work" and named him the "godfather of cannabis research."

Yet despite this acclaim, research into the pharmacological and therapeutic applications of CBD has often been overshadowed by another compound from the same cannabis plant—tetrahydrocannabinol, or THC.

As the psychoactive component of cannabis, THC attracted substantial research and public interest during the latter half of the twentieth century due to its mind-altering effects. While Mechoulam had advanced the study of CBD into the scientific arena, it was THC that dominated the discourse around cannabis, for better or worse.

Because of the stigma surrounding the psychoactive properties of THC, the legal landscape for cannabis and its compounds, including CBD, was largely restrictive for decades. This stifled research and public access. In 1970, the Controlled Substances Act in the United States categorized all forms of cannabis as Schedule I drugs, placing them among substances considered to have a high potential for abuse and with no accepted medical use.

But this classification was premature. Later research, building upon Mechoulam's foundation, revealed incredible therapeutic potential for CBD, which has no psychoactive properties. Yet this institutionalized stigma significantly hampered research into this therapeutic potential of cannabinoids and cemented the unfortunate (and wholly unnecessary) social stigma surrounding cannabis for many decades.

Yet as the twenty-first century began, a slow but crucial shift in attitudes toward cannabis and CBD began to take shape. Instigated by pioneering pharmacological researchers, the potential therapeutic benefits of CBD— initially surrounding its anti-inflammatory and analgesic effects—began to prove too potent for the ever-aggressive pharmaceutical industry to ignore. Researchers around the world were discovering simultaneously that CBD could potentially be used to alleviate pain and reduce inflammation, making it a promising option for patients suffering from chronic pain and various inflammatory conditions.

But beyond pain and inflammation management, one of the most significant breakthroughs in CBD research was the discovery of its potential as a treatment for epilepsy. In 2013, the groundbreaking case of six year-old American Charlotte Figi was published in the medical journal *Epilepsy & Behavior*. As an infant, Charlotte had been diagnosed with Dravet syndrome—a particularly severe form of epilepsy—and began experiencing up to 300 grand mal seizures every week. But upon taking CBD (her mother's idea), her seizures reduced in frequency by 99 percent—from 300 a week to less than one, on average.

Predictably, Charlotte's story set off a firestorm of media coverage, prompting a flurry of interest in further research into the therapeutic benefits of CBD by leading pharmaceuticals around the world. Her story was covered extensively by media outlets such as CNN and the *New York Times*. The documentary *Weed* by CNN's Dr. Sanjay Gupta also featured Charlotte's journey and her experience with CBD.

Understandably, this significant potential application of CBD generated considerable and increasingly urgent interest within the medical community and provided a new treatment avenue for epilepsy patients who had not responded to conventional treatments. What had been an interesting possibility now became a worldwide race to develop and trial life-changing (and possibly life-saving) CBD-based therapies for seriously ill patients.

Furthermore, the turn of the millennium also saw a surge in anecdotal evidence supporting the therapeutic benefits of CBD. Increased commercial availability in particular markets around the world—countries that had not blanket-banned cannabis-related therapies—began to yield encouraging stories of personal experiences with CBD about its efficacy for managing various health conditions and improving quality of life. These personal accounts, while not scientific evidence, contributed to the growing public interest in CBD and its potential health benefits.

Preliminary studies were also conducted during this period, which painted CBD as a promising natural remedy for a variety of conditions. These initial investigations provided a much-needed scientific basis for the anecdotal evidence, further legitimizing CBD as a potential therapeutic agent.

Eventually, the general public began to see CBD as more than just as a derivative of the controversial cannabis plant. CBD research grew into a distinct area of study, both by pharmacological and medical practitioners and by persons around the world experiencing improvements to their health and well-being through experimentation with the compound. This shift in perception began to seriously challenge the longstanding prejudices against cannabis and its derivatives, marking a significant change in how society viewed these substances.

However, it's worth noting that while this shift in perception was significant, it was also gradual. Changing societal attitudes toward substances like cannabis and CBD is a slow process, often taking years or even decades. But the turn of the millennium marked the beginning of this change, setting the stage for the burgeoning interest in CBD that ultimately led to landmark legislation in the 2010s that, to put it bluntly, changed everything.

The 2014 Farm Bill, passed with strong majorities in both houses of Congress and signed by President Obama on February 7, 2014, introduced a critical legal distinction between hemp, which is cannabis with a THC content of less than 0.3%, and marijuana, which is cannabis containing higher levels of THC. This distinction was of paramount importance for the research and sale of CBD, as it permitted the legal cultivation of hemp. This, in turn, allowed for the extraction and sale of CBD that was derived from hemp. To call the bill a game changer for the industry is an understatement.

Building upon the foundation laid by the 2014 Farm Bill, the 2018 Farm Bill—enacted into law on December 20, 2018—went a step further. It legalized hemp cultivation at the federal level, which forbade any states from issuing their own bans. Although hemp production had already begun to take hold across the U.S., this new legislation created the kind of certainty the CBD industry needed to attract significant levels of investment. The results? The CBD industry grew exponentially between 2014 and 2024, and it is now expected to grow at a CAGR of more than 15 percent over the next decade.

Clearly, the market was eager to delve into the vast potentials that CBD had to offer. For years, the exploration and expansion of the CBD space had been significantly hampered by unnecessary and stringent government regulations. But as these legal barriers gradually crumbled under the pressure of shifting societal attitudes and scientific breakthroughs, the floodgates opened for a wave of researchers, entrepreneurs, and innovators eager to meet the growing consumer interest in CBD. Seizing the newfound opportunity, they rushed to develop a diverse range of CBD-infused products to cater to different consumer needs and preferences.

This resulted in a veritable explosion of CBD products on the market. Oils and tinctures were among the first to appear, offering consumers an easy and versatile way to incorporate CBD into their daily routines. These could be taken sublingually for quick absorption or added to food or drink for a more gradual effect.

Next came a flood of CBD-infused edibles—everything from gummies and chocolates to teas and coffees—which made CBD consumption as simple and enjoyable as having a snack or sipping a warm beverage.

Topical CBD products also began to gain traction—creams, balms, and lotions that could be applied directly to the skin. They were particularly popular among consumers seeking localized relief from pain or inflammation or for skin care purposes.

But as with every new market, rapid growth and expansion bring a host of new challenges. While the farm bills and the resulting boom in CBD availability signaled the burgeoning acceptance and demand for CBD products, industry insiders watched as the proliferation of products outpaced the growth of a reasonable and consumer-friendly regulatory framework. The quality and efficacy of CBD products varied greatly, leading to a market that was as confusing as it was diverse.

CBD consumers were suddenly faced with a wide range of products of varying quality. This made it challenging to determine the quality of these items. While many CBD products were of high quality and produced by reputable manufacturers, others were questionable, created by entities looking to capitalize on the

CBD trend with no regard for consumer safety or product effectiveness.

The lack of regulations also meant that there was no requirement for manufacturers to test their products for potency or contaminants. This sometimes led to alarming situations in which consumers could unknowingly purchase and consume subpar, or even harmful, products. This situation underscored the urgent need for standardization across the industry. To ensure consumer safety and trust, it became clear that standards needed to be established for the production and testing of CBD products.

Beyond standardization, there was also a dire need for quality assurance. Consumers needed to be confident that the products they were purchasing were safe and effective and that they contained the advertised amount of CBD. This called for the development of rigorous testing protocols and the establishment of quality assurance programs to verify the quality and potency of CBD products.

The situation also highlighted the need for consumer education. With so many new CBD products on the market, making an informed choice was a daunting task for many consumers. CBD was changing lives; there was no longer any doubt about that. Yet there remained a pressing need to educate consumers about the basics of CBD, including its potential benefits and risks, how to choose a quality product, and how to use it safely.

The rapid expansion of the CBD industry, while a testament to the increasing acceptance of CBD and the success of pioneering researchers to expand access to this therapeutic compound, revealed significant needs for a better way forward—one that would ensure the long-term health and credibility of the industry.

This is where the Corganics story begins.

2

THE VISIONARIES BEHIND THE IDEA

—⁂—

At the heart of every transformative movement lies a particular kind of visionary.

Visionaries are built differently. They stand out from the crowd. They're not in the game for profits or to retire early to a quiet Italian villa. They're not driven by insatiable greed for more money or a quick, comfortable exit or IPO. They're not impartial quantitative analysts exploiting some elusive, hard-to-find arbitrage opportunity that requires a degree in advanced statistics to understand.

A truly transformative visionary—the rare person who, almost alone, moves society's needle—is motivated by something far deeper and more profound.

Visionaries possess the extraordinary capacity to shift the course of societal norms and expectations almost single-handedly. They are the guiding lights whose vision and passion usher in transformative change across teams, organizations, and cultures. They have the audacious courage to challenge the status quo. What sets them apart and fuels their drive is not mere ambition or a desire for recognition. Instead, they are driven by something far deeper, more profound, and more intimate. Their motivation stems from an inner reservoir of passion and conviction, a resolute belief in their ideas, and an unwavering commitment to making a meaningful impact on the world.

Consider Steve Jobs and his vision for truly user-friendly technology, manufactured and delivered at scale to households (and into pockets) around the world. Or Sara Blakely, who transformed the fashion industry with her invention of Spanx, making comfortable shapewear accessible to millions. Or Oprah Winfrey revolutionizing daytime television with a new conversational format that brought the most delicate societal issues to the forefront and mainstream. Or Jeff Bezos delivering more than three million packages to American households every single day, overhauling the way we think about what, how, and when to buy the things we need.

For these kinds of visionaries, numbers are secondary—they always were, and they always will be.

That's because for these kinds of visionaries, the true mission is always personal.

Enter Chad Collins and Reggie Gatewood and their audacious vision for setting the standard in cannabinoid (CBD) therapy.

For decades, the pair worked as senior managers in the hyper-competitive pharmaceutical industry—a dog-eat-dog world characterized by fierce and intense competition for market share. In this industry, the relentless race for innovation clashes with long-standing norms and politics surrounding regulatory compliance and industry standards. This whirlpool of competing forces, while playing an important role in maintaining ethical standards and patient safety, can stifle the creative energies that fuel the kind of bootstrap innovation that drives groundbreaking developments hailing from anywhere outside the board-approved strategic plan.

Ask anyone who's worked at high levels in the pharmaceutical industry, and you'll get the same feedback—the cutthroat competitive business environment that characterizes "big pharma's" strategic planning (which is often responsible for boosting shareholders' already sky-high expectations) routinely pushes hard against guidelines designed by authorities who work within the confines of a regulatory environment that is too often highly politicized. This creates situations in which success in the industry is about perfecting the art of balancing a pressure campaign against established norms and boundaries while maintaining absolute professionalism and an unyielding commitment to product quality.

The fact is that it's easy to get lost in the pharmaceutical world. The pharmaceutical development workflow is a heavy grindstone, and competition means there's little time to step back and scan the horizon for a better path forward. Long research and development, clinical trial, and regulatory approval timelines can make the bottom-line impact of day-to-day improvements hard to see and even harder to justify.

But in the 2010s, Collins and Gatewood got their heads above water often enough to see the explosive potentials of cannabinoid therapy as a groundbreaking therapeutic agent.

Whereas some of this had to do with research and development they'd observed on the exciting new compound, much of their exposure to the potentials of cannabinoid therapy as a therapeutic agent was, according to them, a matter of fortunate timing.

"We happened to be working on a top five global pharmaceutical company's brand that had done research in the cannabinoid therapy space," recounted Collins in a February 2024 interview. "It was still early, and it was preliminary. But it was clear that something big was going on with cannabinoid and CBD therapy in our company and others—it was just a matter of time."

"It was in 2019 before leaving our organizations when we really started doing some due diligence about the CBD marketplace," shared Collins, reflecting in the same interview on the beginnings of his and Gatewood's ongoing journey in the CBD space. "We both had significant experience working at a leading global pharmaceutical company, and we'd both seen that company's slow-but-steady work with cannabinoid therapy and CBD over the prior decade. So this wasn't just a pie-in-the-sky idea for us—we understood cannabinoid and CBD, as did many in the pharmaceutical industry, although we had serious misgivings about how it was being developed, marketed, and used in the retail channel."

But beyond their professional experience with CBD, the pair's interest in the compound was magnified by personal experiences that underscored the growing need for alternative therapeutic options—especially in the area of pain management.

Collins recalled, "From a personal standpoint, the passion started with my disabled, decorated Vietnam veteran father. As he got older, he began having a lot of surgeries and was being prescribed a load of different medications, including opioids, to help him function and keep him comfortable. But it was all so much, maybe too much. At a certain point, he didn't want to be on all of those medications because of the terrible side effects that they have, which can really diminish your quality of life."

Collins wrote a bestselling book about his father titled *Run to the Fire: The True Story of Rick Collins*. It's an exhilarating account of Rick Collins' incredible life. A Vietnam veteran whose body was scarred by battle, Rick returned home to face extreme tragedy and loss. He set a remarkable standard of endurance, faithfulness, and sacrifice, becoming an unlikely superhero. Rick rescued those in need, fought for the voiceless, served his community with dedication, and changed the world around him, leaving a legacy for generations to come. His story will inspire and challenge you to be the kind of person who, when faced with impossible odds, will run to the fire. But it's also the story that represents many other people who are in pain.

Sadly, and unfortunately, this narrative is far too common in our modern world. The adverse effects that traditional medications, especially opioids, can have on patients are often so severe that they compete with the very conditions these drugs are supposed to combat. In fact, according to the National Institutes of Health, more than 1,000 people visit the emergency room every day in the United States because of opioid-related complications. Furthermore, the Centers for Disease Control and Prevention estimates that the total economic burden of prescription opioid misuse in the U.S. is $78.5 billion a year—this includes the costs of healthcare, lost productivity, addiction treatment, and criminal justice involvement. Some of these drugs have even given rise to entire subsets of medications specifically developed to alleviate these debilitating side effects.

For decades, the pharmaceutical industry has grappled with this growing problem, increasingly at the behest of activists and government officials sounding alarms about just how dangerous these medications can be. But success has been limited. The harsh reality is that these synthetic drugs, while designed to alleviate pain and discomfort, often lead to paralyzing side effects and even crippling, lifelong addiction.

"This is no secret," said Collins. "It's becoming increasingly clear that our society's approach to medicine including pain, sleep, and anxiety needs a paradigm shift toward more holistic and natural treatments. This isn't a cure-all for everything. But it's a change that needs to happen, and that really should have happened decades ago."

Collins and Gatewood's extensive professional background and years of experience in the pharmaceutical industry empowered them with a unique and highly nuanced perspective on the untapped potential of CBD.

Having spent considerable time in the field, they had a deep understanding of the industry's complexity and what caused the development of this compound to be so slow and cumbersome.

But it wasn't so much development in CBD therapies that they set out to revolutionize as it was the way the compound was being manufactured, marketed, and sold to the people who are seeking and need it as an option.. In the late 2010s, the duo observed a significant shift in patient behavior.

"After CBD was legalized at the state and federal level, patients, in an effort to explore alternatives to their usual prescriptions, started to explore cheaper retail CBD products," explained Gatewood. "We started to see this happen in a very significant way." As any informed onlooker would, Collins and Gatewood were quick to identify the inherent risk in this trend.

The problem, as they saw it, was that these patients were venturing out into an unregulated retail space. In this unpredictable environment, Gatewood lamented, "Consumers don't know exactly what they're getting, and their experience with CBD is, too often, sadly muddied by sub-par products and ineffective regimens."

This stark realization brought to light the urgent need for intelligent oversight and regulation in the CBD space. The Farm Bill of 2018 had given investors the confidence they needed to pour resources into the CBD space. But the legislative work was only half the battle. Once legalized, it was time for on-the-ground innovators and visionaries to make the CBD market work for consumers.

This prompted a vision, a mission, to professionalize the CBD industry. If Collins and Gatewood could ensure CBD's safety, verify its efficacy in a public and professional way, and guarantee its accessibility to patients with conditions that CBD is proven to help alleviate, they'd completely revolutionize this space. That much was clear. And they aimed to accomplish this through a healthcare-oriented focus—one that prioritized the needs of patients and ensuring that they could reap the benefits of CBD without ever compromising on product safety or quality.

"CBD is a healthcare product, plain and simple," noted Collins. "It has immense benefits for the right kind of patients. There is no reason why this compound should not be available, accessible, and safe from top to bottom for everyone who might benefit from it."

But launching such a venture was no quick decision. It involved a significant pivot from their established careers in pharmaceuticals to the uncertain waters of the burgeoning, and often-misunderstood, CBD industry. As Collins articulated, "We left strategic jobs with responsibility for teams with hundreds of people to make this happen by bringing Corganics to life. I love the quote, 'Leadership is the ability to translate vision into reality.' I believe Reggie and I are doing just that."

It was a leap of faith, but not into the dark. Informed by decades of experience and a steady commitment to doing things the right way, Collins and Gatewood's vision was underpinned by a conviction in the transformative potential of CBD and a shared personal and professional commitment to bridging the gap between natural therapies and mainstream healthcare.

Indeed, not long after deciding to launch Corganics, Collins had an experience that illuminated their best path forward. During a lunch meeting with a venture capitalist involved in hemp farming, he posed a pointed question that would pivot their course: "Why doesn't anybody go and make their sales channel through healthcare professionals to give them that answer?" Collins immediately picked up the phone to discuss this with Gatewood based on their history and joint admiration of each other's skills. This question further confirmed the pair's informed observations about the healthcare industry's need for a trusted CBD brand. It encapsulated the essence of their vision—to create a product that could seamlessly integrate into the massive U.S. healthcare ecosystem, offering patients a natural, effective alternative to conventional medications.

As we dive deeper into the origins and motivations of these two visionaries, it becomes increasingly evident that this journey was not just about launching a product. It was also about challenging a healthcare status quo, advocating for patient autonomy in treatment choices, and ultimately reshaping the landscape of wellness and healthcare with a promising product that has really only just gotten started. The story is a testament to the power of innovation, empathy, and unwavering dedication to improving patient outcomes through the therapeutic potential of CBD.

3

THE BIRTH OF CORGANICS

"It was January 2020 when we officially incorporated the company," Collins recalled. "We did that right here in Dallas, Texas, where we were both based."

And in many ways, Texas is a fitting place for an endeavor like Corganics. Renowned for its increasingly dynamic business ecosystem, Texas fosters a culture that celebrates innovation and enterprise, drawing in ambitious entrepreneurs eager to make their mark. The state's supportive business environment, characterized by favorable tax policies, access to venture capital, and robust infrastructure, provides a solid foundation for startups to thrive. Its deep-rooted spirit of independence and resilience permeates its entrepreneurial landscape, inspiring risk-taking and creativity—two things needed to make a mark in an industry as overly ripe as the CBD market. With a rich and growing tapestry of industry expertise, diverse talent pools, and collaborative networks, Texas offers fertile ground for cultivating ground-breaking ventures.

But Texas isn't core to Corganics' formation. This venture, and all it represents, is bigger than any one place.

At the heart of Corganics' formation was the founders' shared history in the pharmaceutical industry and the wealth of collective experience they brought to the table. Their extensive professional backgrounds provided them with a unique and insightful vantage point—one not shared by many, or even most, founders and innovators across the burgeoning CBD industry by that time. From this perspective, they could critically assess the CBD market's shortcomings and identify opportunities for improvement, being familiar with what success looks like in the pharmaceutical industry.

Collins and Gatewood had spent decades working in the pharmaceutical sector, acquiring deep expertise in such areas as quality control, regulatory compliance, and product development. This background gave them a distinct advantage when entering the CBD market. They understood the importance of rigorous testing and validation, ensuring that products meet high standards of safety and efficacy. This allowed them to recognize that many existing CBD products lacked consistency and reliability, which were critical factors for consumer trust and industry credibility.

Their pharmaceutical experience enabled them to see the potential for applying stringent quality assurance practices to CBD products. They knew that the CBD market was growing rapidly but was also marked by a lack of standardization and oversight. Many companies were producing CBD products without adequate testing, leading to issues with potency, purity, and labeling accuracy. The founders saw an opportunity to differentiate Corganics by prioritizing these aspects and offering products that consumers could trust.

In their previous roles, the founders were accustomed to working within strict regulatory frameworks. They brought this mindset to Corganics, understanding that clear and transparent processes were essential for building a reputable brand. They implemented rigorous quality control measures, from sourcing raw materials to final product testing. This approach not only ensured compliance with existing regulations but also positioned Corganics as a leader in advocating for higher industry standards.

Additionally, their pharmaceutical backgrounds provided them with insights into effective product formulation and delivery methods. They applied this knowledge to develop CBD products that were not only high quality but also innovative and effective. By leveraging their expertise, they aimed to create formulations that maximized the therapeutic benefits of CBD, addressing specific consumer needs and health concerns.

The founders' deep understanding of the pharmaceutical industry also informed their business strategy. They knew that success depended on more than just product quality; it required building strong relationships with stakeholders, including suppliers, regulatory bodies, and customers. They emphasized transparency and education, providing consumers with clear information about their products, including the benefits, potential side effects, and the importance of proper dosage.

"Because Reggie and I have a wealth of experience as senior pharmaceutical leaders," Collins said, reflecting on their decision to enter the CBD industry, "we made a conscious decision that we could bring a healthcare-oriented focus and professionalize the CBD industry." This strategic decision was not merely a business move. It was a commitment to raising the bar for the standard of CBD products available to patients. They aimed to leverage their deep industry insights and knowledge to ensure their offerings met and exceeded the highest quality standards.

The early days of Corganics were characterized by a rigorous process of product development and partner vetting. Collins and Gatewood were determined to differentiate its offerings from the flurry of mostly unregulated CBD products flooding the market at the time—a slipshod environment that, for better or worse, manufacturers in the CBD space had gotten used to.

So in the earliest days, the pair spent most of their time searching for manufacturing partners who aligned with their vision of both quality and transparency. They understood that establishing a reliable and trustworthy supply chain was critical to their success. They meticulously evaluated potential partners, scrutinizing their production processes, quality control measures, and commitment to transparency. This was no small feat, given the multitude of suppliers in the rapidly expanding CBD market, many of whom were more interested in quick profits than in long-term quality and compliance.

Gatewood noted, "The first six months we spent on a search. We carefully vetted potential manufacturing partners that could meet the same standards that we expected in the pharmaceutical industry, but applied to CBD products." This insistence on quality underscores the meticulous approach Corganics takes to ensure that their products would be, from the very beginning, synonymous with reliability and trust.

Corganics began by identifying potential partners who had a proven track record in the pharmaceutical or nutraceutical industries. They believed that companies with experience in these sectors would be more likely to adhere to stringent quality standards and regulatory requirements. This initial filtering process narrowed their list of candidates and also ensured that they were considering only the most reputable and reliable manufacturers.

The founders then conducted detailed audits of these potential partners' facilities. They visited manufacturing sites to observe the production processes firsthand, looking for signs of best practices in quality control and safety. They examined how raw materials were sourced, stored, and processed, paying close attention to cleanliness, consistency, and documentation. These visits were crucial in assessing whether a partner could meet the high standards Corganics intended to set.

During these audits, Collins and Gatewood also evaluated the partners' testing protocols. They knew that rigorous testing was essential to ensure the purity, potency, and safety of their CBD products. They looked for partners who conducted comprehensive testing at multiple stages of the production process, from raw material intake to final product packaging. They preferred those who used third-party laboratories to validate their results, adding an extra layer of transparency and credibility.

In addition to quality control, transparency was a key criterion in the vetting process. Collins and Gatewood sought partners who were willing to share detailed information about their production methods and testing results. They wanted to work with manufacturers who were open about their practices and who could provide verifiable documentation. This transparency was essential for building trust with consumers and differentiating Corganics from other brands in the market.

The search for the right partners was a time-consuming and often challenging endeavor. Collins and Gatewood faced numerous setbacks and disappointments along the way. Some potential partners failed to meet their stringent standards, while others were unwilling to provide the level of transparency required. However, these challenges only strengthened their resolve to find partners who truly aligned with their vision.

Once they identified suitable manufacturing partners, the next step was to develop the product formulations. Collins and Gatewood leveraged their pharmaceutical backgrounds and network with highly respected physicians and researchers to create formulations that were not only effective but also consistent and safe. They collaborated closely with their manufacturing partners to refine these formulations, ensuring that each product met their high standards for quality and efficacy.

The product development phase involved extensive testing and iteration. Collins and Gatewood were meticulous in their approach, conducting multiple rounds of testing to fine-tune the formulations. They gathered feedback from early testers, made necessary adjustments, and repeated the process until they were confident in the final products. This rigorous development process ensured that Corganics' offerings were of the highest quality and could stand out in a crowded market.

Throughout this period, Collins and Gatewood maintained a strong focus on compliance with regulatory standards. They closely monitored changes in regulations and ensured that their products met all legal requirements. This proactive approach helped them navigate the complex regulatory landscape of the CBD industry and positioned Corganics as a brand committed to safety and compliance.

On top of this, the pair's strategic decision to focus on healthcare professionals as their primary sales channel testifies to their desire to integrate CBD into mainstream patient care. This compound, they say, is too valuable to be left to the fringes of the pharmaceutical space. This approach was not only innovative but also reflects Corganics' broader mission to provide patients with safe, effective alternatives to traditional medications in a professional and transparent way.

"We wanted to bridge the gap with patients who are looking for those alternatives to prescriptions," Collins articulated, highlighting the gap in the market that Corganics aimed to fill.

Over the next eighteen months, Corganics transitioned from an ambitious concept to a tangible business entity. But as any founder knows, this process of early growth comes with new challenges that test even the most enthusiastic founder's resolve.

For Collins and Gatewood, specifically, this meant coming face to face with the multifaceted challenges of establishing a foothold in the fresh, competitive, and complex CBD market. The initial period following the company's inception was a critical time of careful strategic navigation, marked by efforts to solidify Corganics' unique position in the industry. The founders' backgrounds in pharmaceuticals played a pivotal role, guiding their approach to product development, regulatory compliance, and market entry with a level of professionalism and rigor seldom seen in the nascent CBD market.

During these eighteen months, Collins and Gatewood faced numerous obstacles that required them to be both innovative and resilient. One of the first challenges was securing the necessary funding to move their vision forward. They spent countless hours meeting with potential investors to present their business plan and highlight the unique value proposition of Corganics. Their pharmaceutical experience was a significant selling point, as it assured investors that they had the expertise needed to navigate the complexities of the CBD market. Despite the rigorous scrutiny from investors, Collins and Gatewood successfully raised the capital needed to fund their initial operations.

With funding in place, the next challenge was to establish a robust supply chain. The founders were meticulous in selecting suppliers who could provide high-quality, consistent raw materials. This was no easy task in an industry where standards varied widely. They traveled extensively to meet with potential suppliers, conduct inspections, and negotiate terms. Each decision was made with careful consideration to ensure that the supply chain would support their commitment to quality and transparency. This process took several months but ultimately resulted in partnerships with suppliers who shared their vision and standards.

Simultaneously, Collins and Gatewood focused on building a strong team. They sought out individuals who not only had the necessary skills and experience but also shared their passion for the company's mission. Recruiting talent in a new industry was challenging, as there was a limited pool of candidates with relevant experience. However, the founders' dedication to creating a positive and impactful workplace attracted professionals who were excited to be part of something groundbreaking. They built a team that was as committed to excellence as they were, fostering a culture of collaboration and innovation.

Regulatory compliance was another significant hurdle. The CBD industry was, and still is, subject to a complex and evolving regulatory landscape. Collins and Gatewood had to stay abreast of changing laws and regulations, ensuring that Corganics' products met all legal requirements. They invested in legal and regulatory expertise, working closely with consultants to navigate this challenging environment. Their pharmaceutical background was invaluable here, as they were already familiar with the importance of compliance and had experience working within stringent regulatory frameworks.

Product development was a cornerstone of Corganics' strategy. The founders were committed to creating products that were not only effective but also safe and reliable. They applied their pharmaceutical knowledge to develop formulations that maximized the benefits of CBD while ensuring consistency and quality. This involved extensive research and development, multiple rounds of testing, and constant refinement. They worked closely with their manufacturing partners to ensure that every product met their high standards. This rigorous approach to product development helped differentiate Corganics from competitors and built a strong foundation for the brand.

Marketing and branding were also critical during this period. Collins and Gatewood understood that to succeed in a crowded market, Corganics needed a strong and distinctive brand identity. They invested in market research to understand consumer needs and preferences, using this information to craft a compelling brand story. They emphasized the unique aspects of their products, such as pharmaceutical-grade quality and transparency. Their marketing efforts were focused on building trust with physicians, healthcare professionals, and their patients, highlighting their commitment to safety, efficacy, and ethical practices. These efforts paid off, as Corganics quickly gained a reputation for quality and reliability.

Distribution was another area where the founders faced significant challenges. They needed to establish a network that could efficiently get their products into the hands of patients. This involved negotiating with distributors, setting up logistics, and ensuring that their products were available in key markets. They faced competition from established brands and had to prove that their products were worth stocking. Through persistence and strategic partnerships, they succeeded in building a distribution network that supported their growth.

Healthcare professional education was an ongoing effort. Collins and Gatewood realized that many healthcare professionals and patients were unfamiliar with CBD and its potential benefits. They invested in educational initiatives to inform HCPs and patients about the science behind their products, the importance of quality control, and how to use CBD safely and effectively. This included creating informative content, hosting webinars, and engaging with the healthcare community through various channels. Their dedication to education helped build a loyal customer base and positioned Corganics as a trusted source of information in the CBD market.

One of the primary challenges was distinguishing Corganics in a market flooded with products of variable quality and uncertain efficacy. Collins and Gatewood were acutely aware of the pitfalls that plagued the CBD industry, particularly the lack of regulation and the presence of products that could potentially harm rather than help patients. Collins noted, "The problem was they're going out to an unregulated retail space, and in that unregulated retail space, you don't know what you're getting." This observation underscored the need for a product that healthcare professionals could trust and recommend with confidence, a principle that would become a cornerstone of Corganics' mission.

This entailed an exhaustive search for manufacturing partners who shared their commitment to quality and could deliver a product that was both effective and compliant with stringent regulatory standards. "We probably talked to maybe a hundred different manufacturers until we found one that we can't disclose; that's kind of our trade secret, but it's more aligned with what you would find a partner in pharma to be," one founder remarked. This meticulous vetting process was indicative of Corganics' dedication to setting a new standard in the CBD industry.

One early milestone came in November 2021, when Corganics received a Series A seed investment from Altacrest Capital. While the investment was significant, this infusion of capital wasn't just about financial growth. The big picture is that it symbolized the market's recognition of Corganics' dedication to expanding clinical product offerings and enhancing the company's branding strategy as a professional and high-quality CBD manufacturer.

The investment not only fueled the expansion of Corganics' CBD product portfolio, but also the ability to engage healthcare professionals at medical conferences. This strategic investment move broadened Corganics' reach into the realm of the healthcare space, catering to a diverse range of healthcare professionals, including oncologists, primary care providers, orthopedic surgeons, and more— the deeper, more transparent collaboration that had been exactly the founders' strategy from the beginning.

With the new capital in hand, Collins and Gatewood immediately set to work on launching their operations. This meant expanding their research and development team to accelerate the creation of new and innovative products. They hired additional scientists, researchers, and product developers who shared their vision of high-quality, effective CBD and non-CBD products. This bolstered team allowed Corganics to push the boundaries of what was possible in the industry, ensuring that they stayed ahead of the curve in terms of product offerings and technological advancements.

The Series A investment also enabled Corganics to enhance its manufacturing relationship capabilities. They invested in manufacturers with state-of-the-art equipment and facilities to ensure that their production processes were as efficient and reliable as possible. This upgrade not only increased their production capacity but also allowed for more precise control over product quality. By maintaining rigorous standards and using cutting-edge technology, Corganics could ensure that every product they released met the high expectations of both patients and healthcare professionals.

In addition to product and manufacturing enhancements, Corganics focused on strengthening their supply chain. They established strategic partnerships with reliable suppliers to ensure a consistent and high-quality supply of raw materials. These partnerships were crucial in maintaining the integrity of their products and supporting their commitment to transparency and quality. The founders knew that a robust supply chain was essential for scaling their business and meeting the growing demand for their products.

Marketing and branding efforts received a significant boost from the investment as well. Corganics launched comprehensive marketing campaigns to raise brand awareness and educate healthcare professionals about the benefits of their products. They used various channels, including social media and in practice promotions, to reach a wider audience. The campaigns highlighted the unique qualities of Corganics' products, emphasizing their pharmaceutical-grade quality, rigorous testing, and commitment to transparency. These efforts helped establish Corganics as a trusted and reputable brand in the CBD and pain, sleep, and anxiety management markets.

The founders' long-term vision included fostering deeper collaboration with healthcare professionals. The investment allowed Corganics to strengthen their relationships with key stakeholders in the medical community. They organized educational seminars and workshops to inform healthcare providers about the benefits of their products and how they could be integrated into patient care plans. These initiatives helped build trust and credibility with healthcare professionals, positioning Corganics as a valuable partner in patient care.

Furthermore, Corganics invested in IRB (Institutional Review Board) clinical research to validate the efficacy and safety of their products. They partnered with research institutions including UCLA, the University of

Washington, and the University of Wisconsin and conducted clinical studies to gather data and evidence supporting their product claims. This commitment to scientific research not only reinforced their credibility but also provided valuable insights for future product development. By grounding their products in science, Corganics could confidently share data with healthcare professionals.

As Corganics expanded its reach and influence, Collins and Gatewood remained steadfast in their commitment to quality and transparency. They continued to prioritize the needs of their customers and healthcare partners, ensuring that every decision aligned with their core values. This dedication to excellence earned them a loyal customer base and respect within the industry. The Series A investment was more than just a financial boost; it was a validation of their vision and hard work, propelling Corganics toward a future of sustained growth and success.

The early days of Corganics were also defined by the founders' strategic decision to build relationships with healthcare professionals as the primary channel for their products. This approach was not only innovative but also reflective of Corganics' broader mission to integrate CBD into mainstream healthcare. "We focused on healthcare professionals as our customers. We let them be the filter for patients," Gatewood explained. This strategy underscored a commitment to ensuring that patients received a product that was not only effective but also met the highest standards of safety and quality.

In the last two years, Corganics made huge strides toward deepening these practitioner relationships. The company routinely announced collaboration with some of the most respected and largest healthcare practices in the U.S., including those in orthopedics, oncology, and aesthetics. These partnerships underscored Corganics' reputation for quality and safety, as these major practices chose it as their trusted provider for CBD therapy, aligning with the brand's mission of delivering advanced, medically supervised treatments.

The implementation of these partnerships involved a detailed plan to ensure seamless integration of CBD products into a practice's existing treatment protocols. Corganics worked closely with entire healthcare professional teams to educate them on the benefits and applications of CBD. This included onsite training sessions, webinars, and comprehensive guides on how to incorporate CBD into patient care. The educational component was crucial, as it ensured that healthcare providers were well-informed and confident in recommending CBD as part of their treatment plans.

Marketing efforts and patient collateral designs were ramped up to promote the collaboration within each practice. Joint campaigns were launched to highlight the benefits of the integrated treatments offered by practices and Corganics. These campaigns used various channels, including social media, online platforms, and in-clinic promotions, to reach a broad audience. Testimonials from satisfied patients and endorsements from healthcare professionals were featured prominently, showcasing the positive impact of CBD on overall wellness. This strategic marketing helped raise awareness about the partnership and attracted new practices to Corganics.

In addition to the marketing and educational initiatives, Corganics and practices developed customized procedure, surgical, and wellness protocols and regimens that included Corganics Clinical CBD products tailored to individual patient needs. These regimens were designed to address specific issues, such as the potential to reduce risky prescriptions and enhance recovery, including improved sleep and reduced anxiety. By offering personalized care plans, Corganics and practice partners were able to provide more effective solutions and enhance patient satisfaction. The success of these tailored regimens contributed to the growing trust and loyalty among patients, leading to even more adoption among health-care practices.

The collaboration also opened new avenues for research and development. Corganics and a number of respected research institutions established joint R&D teams in such places as NYU Langone, Rush, Harvard, and Wake Forest to explore further applications of Corganics Clinical CBD. These teams have worked on developing new treatment protocols that could address a wider range of health concerns. The R&D efforts were supported by feedback from patients and healthcare providers, ensuring that the new protocols were aligned with the needs and expectations of current and potential practice partners in the future. This continuous innovation will help keep Corganics, practice partners, and research partners at the forefront of the integration of safe, natural products into the mainstream of medicine.

Progress was fast. The partnership with initial research and adoption among practices had a ripple effect, attracting interest from other healthcare professionals and practice clinics. They saw the success of the Corganics collaboration and were eager to explore similar partnerships. Collins and Gatewood received numerous inquiries from clinics specializing in orthopedics, oncology, dermatology, and primary care, all interested in integrating Corganics' CBD products into their treatment offerings. This interest led to a series of new partnerships, further expanding Corganics' reach and influence in the medical community.

After just two years, the birth of Corganics had proven to be more than the establishment of a new company. It was—and is—the beginning of a movement aimed at transforming the CBD industry entirely. The founders' vision of integrating pharmaceutical-grade quality and rigorous standards into the CBD market was becoming a reality. They had successfully demonstrated that CBD could be a valuable component of medical treatment plans, gaining the trust of healthcare professionals and patients alike. Corganics' commitment to quality, transparency, and patient care set a new benchmark in the industry.

The journey from concept to a thriving business entity was marked by strategic decisions, relentless dedication, and a clear vision. Collins and Gatewood's pharmaceutical background had been instrumental in navigating the complex landscape of the CBD market. Their approach to product development, regulatory compliance, and market entry was characterized by a level of professionalism and rigor seldom seen in the industry. This foundation allowed them to overcome challenges and seize opportunities, positioning Corganics as a leader in the healthcare CBD and wellness space.

Looking ahead, Corganics planned to continue its expansion and innovation. The founders were committed to exploring new partnerships and developing products that addressed a wider range of health concerns. They aimed to further integrate their products into mainstream medical practice, advocating for the benefits of CBD in various areas of health and wellness. The success of their partnerships with leading orthopedic, oncology, and other practices was just the beginning, and they were excited about the future possibilities.

In mid-2023, Corganics embarked on more transformative ventures, partnering with the largest independent orthopedic practice in Texas that is also in the top three nationally, and Texas Oncology, the largest oncology practice in the U.S., as well as some of the most respected dermatology/aesthetic practices. These partnerships aren't just about providing access to cannabinoid therapy, but is about empowering patients with safe, transparent, and effective alternatives for managing orthopedic, oncology, and dermatologic/aesthetic support care conditions.

The collaboration between Corganics and these strategic partners represent a significant step forward in integrating CBD therapies into mainstream medical practice. Strategic partners like these are known for comprehensive and cutting-edge orthopedic, cancer, or dermatology and aesthetic care, and they saw the potential in offering patients an additional natural treatment option. For Corganics, these partnerships provide an opportunity to further their mission of elevating the standards of the CBD industry and ensuring that patients received the highest quality, cleanest, and safest products available in the U.S.

"Our strategic corporate partners across specialties have a reputation for excellence in delivering orthopedic, cancer, and dermatology care, and we're honored to work with them on providing patient access to trusted CBD therapies," said Collins. "By making Corganics' tested and proven therapies available throughout these unrivaled clinics, we're helping patients avoid self-treating with CBD treatments that may be mislabeled or contain harmful contaminants."

The integration of Corganics' products into those landmark practice offerings required meticulous planning and coordination. The partnerships kicked off with a series of educational sessions for medical staff. Corganics provided comprehensive training on the data, benefits, uses, and potential side effects of CBD therapy, ensuring that healthcare professionals were well-informed and confident in recommending these treatments to their patients. This education was crucial, as it bridged the knowledge gap and addressed any skepticism regarding the efficacy and safety of CBD products.

"These partnerships will benefit thousands of patients throughout Texas and beyond who are seeking safe and natural alternative therapies," added Gatewood. "Corganics is committed to working with orthopedic, oncology, and dermatology practices to provide the highest quality and most transparent CBD product options in the market. This level of integrity gives these forward-thinking practices options they can rely on when patients ask about CBD therapies."

Corganics and the leading orthopedic practices have worked together to integrate CBD therapies into treatment protocols for various orthopedic conditions including pre- and post-surgery. This included developing specific guidelines on how and when to incorporate CBD products into patient care plans whether in acute or long-term settings. Corganics learned that leading practices were eager to have CBD offered as a promising alternative or complement to traditional treatments. The focus was on providing patients with a natural approach that could potentially reduce reliance on prescription medications and other pharmaceuticals with significant side effects.

To ensure the highest standards of quality and safety, Corganics implemented rigorous testing and quality control measures for all products available through these practices. Each batch of CBD products underwent comprehensive testing for potency, purity, and contaminants. This transparency in testing and results reassured both the medical professionals and their patients about the safety and efficacy of the products being used. Corganics provided detailed documentation and lab reports, which were made accessible to staff and patients, further building trust and credibility.

These partnerships also involve a patient education component. Corganics and these strategic partners jointly developed informational materials and resources to help patients understand the benefits and proper use of CBD therapies. This included brochures, online content, and in-clinic seminars where patients could ask questions and learn about CBD from medical professionals. The goal was to empower patients with knowledge, helping them make informed decisions about their treatment options.

Moreover, the collaboration opened up new avenues for clinical research. Building credibility by partnering with some of the most respected and largest practices in orthopedics has attracted the most reputable research institutions wanting to conduct research with Corganics Clinical CBD products. Corganics plans to conduct joint studies to further explore the effectiveness of CBD in treating orthopedic conditions. These studies aim to provide empirical data that could support the broader adoption of CBD therapies in orthopedic care followed by other studies within other specialties. By contributing to the scientific body of evidence, Corganics hopes to influence industry standards and encourage more healthcare providers to consider CBD as a viable treatment option.

The impact of these partnerships was felt quickly. Patients reported positive outcomes, including reduced reliance on prescriptions across a number of issues such as pain, sleep, and anxiety, to name a few. These success stories were shared through various channels, including patient testimonials and case studies within those practices, highlighting the real-world benefits of integrating CBD into care. This positive feedback reinforced the value of these partnerships and encouraged other practices to explore similar collaborations with Corganics.

These types of high level partnerships also positioned Corganics as a leader in the CBD industry, setting a new benchmark for quality and transparency. Their collaboration with a prestigious organization validated their commitment to excellence and their ability to meet the stringent demands of medical professionals. It demonstrated that Corganics was not just a CBD company but also a trusted partner in healthcare, dedicated to improving patient outcomes through innovative and natural therapies.

As Corganics continued to grow, the founders planned to replicate this model of partnership with other medical practices across different specialties. The success served as a blueprint for future collaborations, in which Corganics could bring its expertise to various fields of medicine, from orthopedic, oncology, and dermatology to numerous other specialties to provide patients access to the most trusted version of CBD in the U.S. by healthcare professionals. Each partnership was an opportunity to expand the reach of CBD therapies and showcase their potential to enhance patient care.

Corganics' products undergo rigorous testing in ISO-certified labs and are manufactured in facilities that comply with cGMP (Current Good Manufacturing Practice) standards and the NSF Certified for Sport program. This meticulous process ensures the highest quality and safety standards for their products. Notably, Corganics' clinical CBD therapy products contain no detectable THC, adhering to stringent purity requirements. These products are exclusively available through healthcare professionals or with a referral from a healthcare provider, emphasizing their commitment to medical-grade quality and patient safety.

As one orthopedic physician partner and practice president shared, "Patients are treating themselves with retail CBD products that may or may not have the advertised content. Our practice felt that they deserve access to a product that is safer, higher quality, and cleaner than current retail versions." This statement underscores the growing concern among medical professionals regarding the unregulated nature of many retail CBD products and highlights the necessity for reliable, medically endorsed alternatives.

The story of Corganics' early days is a testament to the power of purpose-driven entrepreneurship. The founders navigated numerous challenges as they transitioned from concept to realization, driven by a steadfast commitment to quality and innovation. Their strategic approach to product development and market entry was instrumental in establishing Corganics as a distinguished entity in the CBD industry. Through their unwavering efforts, Corganics has not only entered the market but has also set new standards for quality, integrity, and innovation, earning the trust and respect of healthcare professionals and patients alike. This journey reflects the founders' dedication to creating products that genuinely improve lives, positioning Corganics as a beacon of excellence in a rapidly evolving market.

4

BRIDGING THE GAP

Corganics' mission is to bridge the gap between healthcare professionals and their patients regarding the understanding and treatment of the Endocannabinoid System (ECS). Patients in the United States are increasingly seeking safe, natural alternatives to prescription medications and are turning to their healthcare providers for opinions and recommendations on such treatments. In response, when Corganics launched its first innovative products in 2022, their offerings swiftly became the most trusted CBD therapies among healthcare professionals across multiple specialties in the United States.

Corganics offers scientifically formulated and physician-advised broad-spectrum CBD products that meet the highest quality standards expected of premium medications. The company's advanced technology and manufacturing capabilities, combined with extensive third-party testing and IRB-approved data, distinguish Corganics' products from retail versions of cannabinoid therapy. Understanding the potential of hemp-based, broad-spectrum cannabinoid therapy, Corganics is committed to expediting its integration into treatment options available to healthcare professionals.

Historically, healthcare professionals have been largely excluded from the conversation surrounding CBD therapy and its potential benefits for their patients. Corganics aims to change this dynamic by educating and reintegrating healthcare professionals as trusted, unbiased sources of information on quality hemp-derived cannabinoid therapy. By doing so, Corganics ensures that healthcare professionals are well-informed about how CBD interacts with the ECS and can confidently discuss these treatments with their patients.

In this way, Corganics is not simply a seller of high-quality CBD products for physicians, but an educator as well. The company's commitment to education is evident in the extensive resources and support they provide to healthcare professionals. Corganics spends as much time in educating as in selling its products, recognizing that informed practitioners are essential to the effective use of cannabinoid therapies. It offers comprehensive training programs, detailed informational materials, and continuous support to ensure that healthcare providers fully understand the science and potential benefits of CBD. This educational approach empowers physicians to make informed decisions and to confidently recommend CBD therapies to their patients. By prioritizing education, Corganics fosters a deeper understanding and acceptance of cannabinoid therapies within the medical community, ultimately enhancing patient care and outcomes.

The research into the potential benefits of cannabinoid therapy is complex, yet much of it centers on the ECS. This is a critical regulatory system in the body responsible for maintaining homeostasis, or balance, within various physiological processes. Understanding how this system works is essential for appreciating the potential impact of cannabinoid therapies.

The ECS comprises several key components: endocannabinoids, endocannabinoid receptors (CB1 and CB2), and enzymes that synthesize and degrade endocannabinoids. Endocannabinoids, such as anandamide and 2-AG, are naturally produced compounds that bind to the body's endocannabinoid receptors. These receptors are distributed throughout the body, including the brain, lungs, liver, intestines, muscles, and bones. The widespread presence of these receptors underscores the ECS's extensive role in regulating bodily functions.

The ECS influences a broad range of physiological processes, including sleep, mood, digestion, and inflammation. When endocannabinoids bind to CB1 and CB2 receptors, they help modulate these processes, contributing to overall health and well-being. For instance, CB1 receptors, primarily found in the brain and central nervous system, are involved in regulating mood, appetite, and pain perception. In contrast, CB2 receptors, located mainly in the immune system and peripheral tissues, play a crucial role in managing inflammation and immune response.

Given its impact on such vital functions, the ECS must function correctly for optimal health. Disruptions or imbalances in the ECS can lead to various health issues, making the potential therapeutic benefits of cannabinoid therapy particularly significant. By targeting the ECS, cannabinoid therapies like those provided by Corganics aim to restore balance and promote homeostasis, offering a natural alternative for managing and improving health outcomes.

CBD is a phytocannabinoid, meaning it is derived from a plant. Although it might be easy to assume that CBD binds to the CB1 and CB2 receptors in the same manner as endocannabinoids, this is not the case. Unlike endocannabinoids, CBD does not directly bind to these receptors. Instead, it exerts its effects on the ECS through more indirect pathways.

When CBD is introduced into the body, it influences the ECS indirectly. One of its primary actions is inhibiting the breakdown of natural endocannabinoids. By preventing their degradation, CBD allows these compounds to remain active in the body for a longer period, enhancing their beneficial effects. This prolonged presence of endocannabinoids helps maintain the ECS's regulatory functions more effectively.

Moreover, CBD can bind to or influence non-cannabinoid receptors, further expanding its range of effects. For instance, CBD interacts with receptors such as serotonin and vanilloid receptors, which play roles in regulating mood, pain perception, and inflammation.

Through these interactions, CBD contributes to a broader spectrum of physiological effects, beyond those mediated by the traditional CB1 and CB2 receptors.

Overall, data suggests that CBD can potentially assist the body in maintaining its optimal state of balance, or homeostasis. By enhancing the function of the ECS and influencing other receptor systems, CBD supports the body's natural ability to regulate various physiological processes, promoting overall health and well-being. This multifaceted approach underscores the therapeutic potential of CBD and its role in integrative healthcare.

Until now, physicians have lacked the education, resources, and supplies necessary to confidently offer CBD products to their patients. This gap in knowledge and access has been a significant barrier, preventing healthcare providers from integrating cannabinoid therapies into their treatment plans. Without comprehensive education, many physicians have been unaware of the scientific evidence supporting CBD's potential benefits and its mechanisms of action within the ECS. Additionally, the lack of reliable resources has made it difficult for healthcare professionals to navigate the complex regulatory landscape and differentiate between high-quality, scientifically validated products and those of dubious origin. Furthermore, limited access to a consistent supply of medical-grade CBD products has hindered their ability to recommend and dispense these therapies to patients in need. As a result, patients seeking natural alternatives have often been left to navigate the CBD market on their own, without the guidance of their trusted healthcare providers.

Addressing these challenges is crucial for bridging the gap between traditional medical practice and the emerging field of cannabinoid therapy, ensuring that patients can benefit from the full potential of CBD under the supervision of knowledgeable and well-equipped physicians. This is why Corganics exists, and it is why the company is experiencing such fast growth.

5

SCALING FOR SUCCESS

With the foundational challenges navigated and a clear vision set, Corganics embarked on a journey of expansion that would not only solidify its place within the CBD industry but also redefine the standards for quality and trustworthiness in the market. The scaling phase for Corganics was marked by strategic moves aimed at broadening its reach, deepening its impact, and ensuring its products were accessible to a wider audience without compromising on the core values that defined its early days.

One of the most significant strides in Corganics' growth trajectory was the establishment of partnerships with key opinion leaders and large practices across the United States. These alliances were instrumental in building the brand's credibility and showcasing the efficacy and safety of its products. "We have quickly attracted some of the largest practices in the country," one founder noted, underscoring the trust and confidence the medical community placed in Corganics. This was a testament to the company's success in bridging the gap between the unregulated CBD market and the rigorous demands of healthcare professionals.

The strategic focus on healthcare professionals as the primary distribution channel was further augmented by Corganics' participation in medical conferences and the development of educational platforms. These efforts were crucial in raising awareness about the benefits of CBD and its potential applications in patient care. "We started building the backend, right? And then we came to market about a year and a half ago with the product into the market," a founder reflected, highlighting the methodical approach to building a strong market presence. This phase of Corganics' growth was not just about selling products; it was also about fostering an informed community of healthcare providers who could confidently recommend CBD to their patients.

Moreover, the emphasis on quality and transparency continued to be a major driving force behind Corganics' expansion. The founders were committed to maintaining the highest standards of product integrity, which involved rigorous testing and quality control measures. "We wanted to make sure that our product, when you match it up against some other retail version, ours is more effective," one founder stated, emphasizing the company's dedication to providing superior CBD products. This commitment to excellence was a key differentiator in the market, setting Corganics apart from competitors and establishing it as a leader in the field.

Corganics' growth was also propelled by its ability to navigate the regulatory landscape with agility and foresight. The company's proactive stance on self-regulation and compliance with emerging guidelines helped mitigate potential barriers to market entry and expansion. "We like to say that we self-regulate as you would had it been an FDA product," a founder mentioned, highlighting the proactive measures taken to ensure product safety and compliance. This strategic approach not only facilitated Corganics' expansion but also positioned it as a model for responsible business practices within the industry.

As Corganics scaled, it remained steadfast in its mission to provide safe, effective, and trustworthy CBD products to patients through healthcare professionals. The company's growth was not measured merely by market share or revenue but by the impact it had on improving patient care and advancing the understanding of CBD's therapeutic potential. Through strategic partnerships, a commitment to quality, and a focus on education, Corganics successfully navigated its scaling phase, emerging as a beacon of innovation and integrity in the CBD industry. The company's journey from a visionary startup to a trusted leader in the field exemplifies the transformative power of dedication, innovation, and a relentless pursuit of excellence.

But growing and scaling a startup is fraught with financial challenges that can make or break the business. One of the most pressing issues is securing adequate funding. In the early stages, many startups rely on personal savings, angel investors, or venture capital. However, as the business grows, the need for more substantial funding becomes critical. This often requires navigating complex investment landscapes, pitching to potential investors, and dealing with the intricacies of equity dilution. Furthermore, managing cash flow becomes increasingly difficult. Balancing operational expenses, payroll, and unexpected costs while maintaining enough liquidity to invest in growth opportunities requires meticulous financial planning and foresight.

Another significant financial challenge is managing profitability and scalability. As startups expand, they often face the dilemma of increasing revenue while controlling costs. Scaling operations, whether through expanding the team, increasing production, or entering new markets, can lead to skyrocketing expenses. Ensuring that the business model is scalable without compromising profitability is a delicate balance. Additionally, startups must invest in infrastructure, technology, and marketing to support growth, which can strain financial resources. Navigating these challenges demands a keen understanding of financial metrics, strategic planning, and the ability to pivot when necessary to ensure long-term sustainability and success.

"The journey to financial stability in a startup often involves navigating through numerous unexpected challenges," said Collins. "For example, Reggie and I didn't pay ourselves for the first two years of founding the company, which was a significant sacrifice. When we finally started to put our product in the market and took on an investment, it marked an important turning point." Initially, Corganics' monthly burn rate was quite high, but over the next two years, they managed to reduce it significantly. This reduction was crucial to reach a breakeven point. Achieving breakeven was a milestone that took nearly two years of diligent effort, from the inception of the company to establishing a market presence. Now they are optimistic about the future and see a lot of upside potential.

Most startups face significant challenges in reaching the breakeven point, with many never achieving it at all. The journey to profitability is often longer and more complex than anticipated, marked by high initial costs, intense competition, and fluctuating market demands. While the entrepreneurial spirit is fueled by innovation and ambition, the financial reality is that sustaining a business requires meticulous planning, persistent effort, and sometimes years of operation before revenues match expenses. Consequently, the owners of most startups must be prepared for the possibility that they might operate at a loss for an extended period, and in some cases, may never achieve financial stability. Fortunately, for Corganics, profitability came much sooner.

Reflecting on the fundraising process, it was indeed the first time the founders raised money for a company they owned. This experience was both challenging and enlightening. Securing that initial investment was a game-changer, enabling them to scale their operations and invest in growth opportunities. Despite the initial high burn rate, the strategic investments and financial discipline paid off, leading them to profitability. Now they are confident that their continued investments will keep them profitable from day one, marking a significant turnaround from their early financial struggles. This journey underscores the importance of resilience, strategic planning, and the willingness to make short-term sacrifices for long-term gains in the startup world.

Fundraising is often a tough experience for many entrepreneurs, filled with challenges and obstacles. However, the Corganics journey has been somewhat different. "From the start," said Collins, "we had physicians and others in the healthcare industry interested in investing because they saw firsthand the impact of what we were doing. While it was flattering, we made the strategic decision to partner with a private equity group."

This decision significantly simplified their world. The private equity group managed their investors, freeing them from the burden of handling a diverse group of physician investors, each with different business perspectives. Although they met with several family offices and venture capitalists, they ultimately chose a private equity group that operated differently from the norm. Unlike typical private equity investments, which often result in the investor taking over 51 percent ownership and operating control, Altacrest took a smaller portion. This arrangement allowed Reggie, Chad, and their partners to retain nearly 80 percent ownership of Corganics, keeping them as the majority shareholders and maintaining control over the company's direction.

Their initial pre-money valuation was $7.2 million, a testament to the potential investors saw in their business. As they prepare for their next round of funding, they anticipate a pre-money valuation of at least $20 million. This growth reflects their strategic decisions and the unique approach they took in managing investments. By maintaining majority ownership and simplifying their investor base, they have positioned Corganics for sustainable growth and continued success. This journey highlights the importance of choosing the right investment partners who align with the business vision and operational strategy, ultimately leading to a more streamlined and effective growth trajectory.

6

VOICES OF TRUST: WHAT CORGANICS' CUSTOMERS SAY

In the evolving landscape of healthcare, the integration of CBD products has become a significant development. Among the myriad options available, Corganics has emerged as a leader in providing high-quality, reliable, and science-backed CBD products. This chapter delves into the transformative power of Corganics' CBD products through the lens of medical professionals who have witnessed firsthand the benefits for their patients. These testimonials highlight the purity, effectiveness, and innovative nature of Corganics' offerings.

As we delve into these testimonials from various medical experts, it's evident that Corganics has earned its trust through consistent performance, rigorous testing, and a dedication to advancing the science of CBD. These endorsements highlight the transformative impact of Corganics' products on patient care and underscore the company's role in setting a new standard in the CBD industry.

The Promise of Purity and Trust

One of the foremost concerns in the realm of CBD products is the assurance of purity and absence of contaminants. Many patients turn to CBD for relief but are often met with products that contain unknown additives, including THC. Dr. Steven Paulson, the founder, chairman, and CEO of Texas Oncology, emphasizes the importance of providing a trusted alternative, stating, "CBD oil is a naturally occurring potent anti-inflammatory, sleep, and anti-anxiety medication with few side effects. We're pleased to offer patients a trusted product that's an effective and safe alternative to taking over-the-counter products with unknown contaminants."

This sentiment is echoed by Dr. Patrick St. Pierre, director of shoulder and elbow surgery at Desert Orthopedic Center, who finds assurance in Corganics' commitment to purity. "Many patients try commercially available CBD products to help ease discomfort, but many of these products contain THC or other contaminants. I can trust Corganics products to provide the purest and best research-proven CBD available on the market," he notes, highlighting the critical role that quality assurance plays in patient care.

Rigorous Testing and Proven Efficacy

Corganics' commitment to rigorous testing and transparency sets it apart from other CBD products on the market. Virali Patel, PharmD, RPh, pharmacy manager at Texas Oncology's Presbyterian Cancer Center Dallas, underscores the importance of data and consistency in medical practice. "I feel confident recommending Corganics Clinical CBD products because they are rigorously tested, and each product has a QR code that takes you to a certificate showing what the products are tested for. Healthcare professionals believe in data, and Corganics CBD softgels are proven to help through an IRB-approved study."

Dr. Brian C. Fuller, an adult reconstruction specialist at OrthoTexas, appreciates Corganics' dedication to clinical research and innovation. He asserts, "I believe addressing the endocannabinoid system is an important aspect of a modern multimodal strategy. Corganics is third-party tested, actively participating in clinical research, and continues to develop improved delivery mechanisms, clearly distinguishing itself from retail CBD alternatives."

Enhanced Bioavailability and Technological Advancements

A standout feature of Corganics' CBD products is its advanced technology aimed at enhancing bioavailability, which ensures that patients receive the maximum benefit from the product. Dr. Shariff K. Bishai of the Detroit Orthopaedic Institute underscores this point, noting, "CBD has become a great alternative for patients in my practice. Knowing that the patient will now be able to absorb more and have increased bioavailability with Corganics CBD is a game changer!"

Brandon Welch, PharmD, founder of Pharmacy Athlete, applauds Corganics for its superior absorption technology, stating, "Corganics CBD products are truly leading the market. Their advanced lipid technology is one of a kind with its superior absorption. What I appreciate most about Corganics is it's backed by science and is third-party tested, keeping the product safe from contaminants and impurities."

Revolutionizing Patient Care and Clinical Practice

The integration of Corganics' CBD products into medical protocols has led to significant improvements in patient care and outcomes. Dr. Asheesh Gupta, an orthopedic surgeon at Centers for Advanced Orthopedics, emphasizes the consistency and efficacy of Corganics' products. "Corganics has differentiated itself as the market leader with research-driven CBD products that are efficacious, THC-free, and have a proven consistency. Our experience has been that their superior products provide trusted consistency and are an invaluable addition to my protocols."

Dr. Ghassan Boghosian, a hip and knee reconstruction specialist at Desert Orthopedic Center, acknowledges the impact of Corganics on his practice, stating, "Medical grade CBD provided by Corganics has been beneficial for my patients. With Corganics CBD, my patients have appreciated their advanced technology and improved quality and consistency versus retail CBD."

A Trusted Partner in Pain Management and Patient Care

For many healthcare professionals, Corganics' CBD products have become indispensable tools in managing patient pain and anxiety. Dr. Mary Lupo, a dermatologist, shares her trust in Corganics: "Many patients discuss with me their desire to try CBD products but are concerned about issues of purity. I also am leery about the bioavailability of retail CBD. I have now been recommending Corganics for two years, and my patients and I are thrilled with their results."

Dr. Steven Sorr, ND, founder and medical director of Source of Health, also speaks to the reliability of Corganics: "As a medical professional, I confidently recommend Corganics CBD products for their unwavering commitment to quality and stringent standardization, ensuring consistent efficacy and safety for patients seeking natural solutions."

Embracing the Future of CBD
with Corganics

The future of CBD in medical treatment is bright, thanks to innovative companies like Corganics. Dr. Brett Smith, a total joint and adult reconstruction specialist at the Andrews Institute, expresses his optimism: "The forever improving technological advances created by Corganics will continue to help our patients—truly amazing. The future is even brighter using Corganics."

Dr. Rod Rohrich, a world-renowned plastic surgeon, also highlights Corganics' role in advancing CBD technology: "Corganics continues to raise the bar for their clinical CBD with science-backed innovation and their new Lipid Technology platform. I've trusted Corganics from the beginning, and so do my patients. With these enhancements, in my opinion, the best has gotten even better."

Testimonials from these esteemed medical professionals underscore the transformative power of Corganics' CBD products in enhancing patient care and offering a trusted, effective alternative to traditional treatments. Their endorsements highlight the significant role that Corganics has played in the medical community, providing products that are not only efficacious but also rooted in rigorous scientific validation and superior quality control. This collective recognition from a diverse group of experts, spanning various specialties from oncology to orthopedics and dermatology, reflects a deep-seated confidence in the ability of Corganics to deliver consistent, reliable, and safe CBD solutions for a wide range of health issues.

Each testimonial serves as a powerful testament to the impact of Corganics' CBD products on the quality of life for patients, demonstrating their ability to alleviate pain, reduce inflammation, and improve overall well-being. The unanimous support from these healthcare professionals highlights Corganics' commitment to maintaining the highest standards of purity and efficacy, setting a benchmark for the CBD industry.

7

VISION FOR THE FUTURE

As Corganics solidified its reputation and expanded its reach, the founders looked to the future with a vision that extended beyond the immediate success of their products. This vision encompassed not only the continued growth of Corganics within the CBD industry but also a broader impact on healthcare, patient care, and the global understanding of cannabinoid therapy. The future, as seen through the eyes of the company's leadership, was one of innovation, education, and an unyielding commitment to improving the lives of patients around the world.

A critical aspect of Corganics' future strategy was the emphasis on education and research. Recognizing the potential of CBD in various medical applications, the founders sought to collaborate with leading research institutions and participate in clinical studies. "We also started to invest in medical conferences ... to make our brand and build brand awareness in that market in their space," one founder shared, highlighting the company's proactive approach to fostering an informed medical community. This commitment to research and education aimed not only to bolster the credibility of Corganics' products but also to contribute to the broader body of scientific knowledge surrounding cannabinoid therapy.

Looking ahead, the founders envisioned Corganics playing a pivotal role in shaping the regulatory landscape for CBD products. With a deep understanding of the complexities of the industry and a track record of self-regulation, Corganics aimed to be at the forefront of advocating for standards that ensure product safety, quality, and efficacy. "We may not have been CBD guys, but we acclimated pretty fast with the healthcare background," a founder stated, reflecting on their journey and the company's potential to influence industry standards. This leadership position in regulatory advocacy was seen as essential for the continued growth of the industry and the protection of consumers.

Moreover, Corganics' future vision included expanding its product line and exploring new markets, always with an unwavering focus on the needs of patients and healthcare professionals. The founders recognized the importance of staying at the cutting edge of cannabinoid science and product innovation to meet the evolving needs of their customers. "We're going right to the source and providing them the ability to refer patients," explained Collins, emphasizing the company's patient-centric approach. This strategy of direct engagement with healthcare professionals and a commitment to meeting their needs and those of their patients was central to Corganics' future growth plans.

The company's vision also included leveraging technology and digital platforms to enhance patient education and access to CBD products. By creating online resources, virtual consultations, and telehealth services, Corganics aimed to make it easier for patients and healthcare providers to access accurate information and high-quality products. This digital transformation was seen as a crucial step in democratizing cannabinoid therapy and ensuring that it reaches those who can benefit from it the most.

Corganics' dedication to social responsibility and community engagement was another cornerstone of its future strategy. The founders believed in giving back to the communities they served and supporting initiatives that promote health and well-being. This included partnerships with nonprofit organizations through their Foundation for Corganics Heroes organization, contributions to medical research, and involvement in local healthcare projects. By aligning their business goals with broader social impact, Corganics aimed to build a legacy of positive change and inspire others in the industry to do the same.

At the heart of Corganics' vision for the future was a commitment to transforming the way patients and healthcare providers perceive and use CBD. The founders saw Corganics not just as a company, but also as a movement toward a future where cannabinoid therapy is fully integrated into mainstream healthcare. This vision was fueled by a belief in the transformative power of CBD and a dedication to making it accessible, safe, and effective for those in need.

As Corganics looks to the future, it does so with a sense of responsibility and a commitment to excellence. The path ahead is seen as an opportunity to continue to innovate, educate, and advocate for the benefits of CBD. Through strategic partnerships, continued investment in research, and a deep commitment to patient care, Corganics is poised to lead the way in the evolving landscape of cannabinoid therapy. The vision for the future is clear: to continue to break new ground, challenge the status quo, and improve the lives of patients worldwide. Corganics stands at the forefront of this journey, ready to navigate the challenges and opportunities that lie ahead with integrity, innovation, and an unwavering focus on health and wellness.

APPENDIX

Corganics® provides broad-spectrum CBD products and comprehensive education to healthcare professionals and their patients. By offering scientifically formulated CBD therapies, Corganics ensures that healthcare providers have access to high-quality, clinically validated products. Alongside these products, Corganics delivers extensive educational resources designed to inform and empower healthcare professionals about the benefits and proper use of cannabinoid therapies. This dual focus on product excellence and education enables healthcare providers to confidently incorporate CBD into their treatment plans, ultimately enhancing patient care and outcomes. Corganics' commitment to education also extends to patients, helping them understand how CBD can be an effective part of their overall wellness strategy. Corganics Clinical CBD products are available exclusively through the healthcare channel.

Corganics Clinical CBD Softgels

Corganics Clinical CBD Softgels offer patients a precise serving of THC-free CBD in a convenient and easy-to-use form. Each softgel is formulated with broad-spectrum hemp extract, providing a comprehensive range of cannabinoids, terpenes, flavonoids, and other beneficial compounds found in hemp. These softgels are crafted using Advanced Lipid Technology (A.L.T.), which enhances CBD's bioavailability, ensuring that the body can absorb it more efficiently.

The daily softgels come in thirty-count bottles, with each softgel containing 30 mg of CBD, totaling 900 mg per bottle. This high-absorption formula is derived from USA-grown hemp, ensuring quality and consistency.

To maintain the highest standards of safety and potency, Corganics conducts rigorous third-party testing on all their products. This testing verifies the content and quality of each softgel, providing healthcare professionals and their patients with a reliable and effective CBD option for their therapeutic needs.

Corganics Clinical CBD Drops

Corganics Clinical CBD Drops provide patients with the potential benefits of Corganics' high-quality CBD in an easy-to-use liquid form. Formulated with broad-spectrum, THC-free hemp extract, these drops contain a rich blend of cannabinoids, terpenes, flavonoids, and other beneficial phytochemicals. These natural compounds work synergistically to support overall wellness, delivering optimal support for the endocannabinoid system.

The drops are made using A.L.T., which enhances CBD's bioavailability and makes it easier for the body to absorb. The formula is unflavored and free of THC, ensuring a pure and clean product. Derived from USA-grown hemp, the CBD drops are created to meet the highest standards of quality and efficacy.

The rapid-absorption formula allows for quick and efficient delivery of CBD, making it an ideal option for patients seeking fast relief. Each batch of Corganics Clinical CBD Drops undergoes rigorous third-party testing to verify potency and safety, ensuring that healthcare professionals can trust the consistency and reliability of the product.

Additionally, the drops are formulated with organic olive oil, further enhancing their quality and providing a smooth and natural carrier for the CBD. This meticulous attention to detail and commitment to excellence makes Corganics Clinical CBD Drops a trusted choice for healthcare providers and their patients.

Corganics Clinical CBD Cream

Corganics Clinical CBD Cream offers patients the therapeutic benefits of a meticulously crafted topical solution, combining broad-spectrum hemp extract with vitamin E, aloe vera, and other beneficial natural ingredients. This unscented, THC-free formula is specifically designed to maximize the topical effects of CBD, providing targeted relief and support for various skin concerns and discomforts.

Each tube of Corganics Clinical CBD Cream contains 250 mg of CBD, with a concentration of 8.3 mg/ml. The broad-spectrum hemp extract used in the cream ensures a rich profile of cannabinoids, terpenes, and flavonoids, all working synergistically to enhance the cream's therapeutic potential. Derived from USA-grown hemp, the CBD used in this product meets the highest standards of quality and purity.

Corganics ensures that every batch of their Clinical CBD Cream undergoes rigorous third-party testing to verify its potency and safety. This commitment to quality and transparency provides healthcare professionals and their patients with the confidence that they are using a reliable and effective product.

The inclusion of vitamin E and aloe vera in the cream further enhances its benefits, promoting skin health and providing soothing, moisturizing effects. By blending these natural ingredients with broad-spectrum CBD, Corganics Clinical CBD Cream offers a holistic approach to topical therapy, making it a trusted choice for patients seeking targeted relief without the presence of THC.